SCIENCE FOR THE FUTURE

INTERNET OF THINGS

by Lisa J. Amstutz

FOCUS
READERS

VOYAGER

www.focusreaders.com

Focus Readers is distributed by North Star Editions:
sales@northstareditions.com | 888-417-0195

Produced for Focus Readers by Red Line Editorial.

Content Consultant: Dr. Sherali Zeadally, Associate Professor, College of Communication and Information, University of Kentucky

Photographs ©: metamorworks/Shutterstock Images, cover, 1; Daisy Daisy/Shutterstock Images, 4–5; Jeff Fusco/Comcast/AP Images, 7; Odua Images/Shutterstock Images, 8–9; Anatoly Vartanov/Shutterstock Images, 11; AndreyPopov/iStockphoto, 12; Steven Senne/AP Images, 15; Denys Prykhodov/Shutterstock Images, 16–17; Tatchaphol/Shutterstock Images, 19; vasabii/Shutterstock Images, 21; Elaine Thompson/AP Images, 22–23; selimaksan/iStockphoto, 25; Kwangmoozaa/iStockphoto, 26; Jag_cz/Shutterstock Images, 28–29; XXLPhoto/Shutterstock Images, 31; Matthias Balk/picture-alliance/dpa/AP Images, 33; Stewart Marsden/iStockphoto, 35; Gorodenkoff/Shutterstock Images, 36–37; Nicescene/Shutterstock Images, 39; Casezy idea/Shutterstock Images, 41; David Paul Morris/Bloomberg/Getty Images, 42–43; peeterv/iStockphoto, 45

Library of Congress Cataloging-in-Publication Data
Names: Amstutz, Lisa J., author.
Title: Internet of things / by Lisa J. Amstutz.
Description: Lake Elmo, MN : Focus Readers, [2020] | Series: Science for the
  future | Audience: Grades 7 to 8. | Includes bibliographical references and index.
Identifiers: LCCN 2019008557 (print) | LCCN 2019011442 (ebook) | ISBN
  9781644930045 (pdf) | ISBN 9781641859189 (ebook) | ISBN 9781641857802
  (hardcover) | ISBN 9781641858496 (pbk.)
Subjects: LCSH: Internet of things--Juvenile literature.
Classification: LCC TK5105.8857 (ebook) | LCC TK5105.8857 .A474 2020 (print)
  | DDC 004.67/8--dc23
LC record available at https://lccn.loc.gov/2019008557

Printed in the United States of America
Mankato, MN
May, 2019

ABOUT THE AUTHOR

Lisa J. Amstutz is the author of more than 100 books for kids. She specializes in topics related to science and agriculture. Lisa's background includes degrees in biology and environmental science. She lives with her family on a small-scale farm in Ohio.

TABLE OF CONTENTS

CHAPTER 1
Working Together 5

CHAPTER 2
IoT History 9

SCIENTIST BIO
Kevin Ashton 14

CHAPTER 3
How the IoT Works 17

CHAPTER 4
All Kinds of Devices 23

CHAPTER 5
Efficient Systems 29

SCIENTIST BIO
Larissa Romualdo Suzuki 34

CHAPTER 6
New Challenges 37

CHAPTER 7
The Future of the IoT 43

Focus on the Internet of Things • 46
Glossary • 47
To Learn More • 48
Index • 48

WORKING TOGETHER

It's Monday morning, and the family is asleep. At six o'clock, the coffee maker turns on. The blinds in each person's bedroom open quietly. Then an alarm goes off. The mother and daughters grab their smartphones. Each person opens an app and chooses her breakfast. Moments later, the toaster pops out pieces of toast with the smiley face design each person picked. The mom pours coffee and asks the refrigerator to order more milk.

Modern kitchens are filled with appliances that can connect to the internet.

Then they all sit down for breakfast, messaging friends on their phones as they eat.

Many devices in a home can connect to the internet. They include thermostats, doorbells, and blinds. Users don't need to be near a device to control it. Instead, they can send commands online. People can even create settings to control the device while they are away.

Several devices can join together to form a **network**. The devices share information. They can work together to perform tasks. For example, sensors could detect when it got dark. Then the home's lights could turn on.

➤ THINK ABOUT IT

Networks let devices send and respond to information. What is one situation where the information a device collects could help another device do its job?

▲ The Internet of Things allows families to link and control many different devices.

All these devices are part of the Internet of Things (IoT). This huge network is made up of all devices that use the internet to share information. The IoT includes smartphones, smart appliances, smart watches, and even smart toys. All these things can send information back and forth. In 2018, the IoT included 20 billion devices around the world. As technology improves, that number continues to grow.

CHAPTER 2

IoT HISTORY

The term *Internet of Things* was first used in 1999. But the idea behind it has been around for much longer. Since the 1800s, people have dreamed of making machines that communicate with one another and with the people who use them. They hoped these machines could make tasks easier. For example, many store owners wanted an automatic way to track their products and prices.

The IoT makes it easier for store owners to manage their businesses.

One key step was the invention of bar codes. A bar code is a series of printed lines. The lines contain coded information that a scanner can read. The scanner sends this information to a cash register or computer.

Grocery stores began using bar codes in the 1970s. Before that time, workers had to enter the price for each item. This task could take a long time. And workers often made errors. In contrast, bar codes showed the prices automatically, saving stores time and money. Bar codes also helped factories track their products. Libraries used them to track books, too.

In the 1980s, scientists began testing the first IoT devices. These early devices were simple. But two key inventions helped IoT technology spread. One was the global positioning system (GPS). This system made it possible to track an object's

People can scan bar codes to access information.

exact location. In 1993, the US government
launched several GPS satellites. These devices
orbit Earth and send out radio signals. An object
with a **GPS receiver** can pick up the signals and
use them to calculate its own location.

 GPS provides directions when a user enters an address.

In 1997, radio-frequency identification (RFID) tags came along. An RFID tag is similar to a bar code. Like bar codes, RFID tags can be scanned and tracked by a computer. RFID readers collect data from the tags and send the data to a computer for processing. Because the tags use radio signals, RFID readers don't need to be able to see a tag to scan it. They just need to be near the tag. Plus, RFID readers can scan many tags at once. GPS and RFID tags made it much easier for companies to track their products.

In 2000, a company produced a refrigerator with a screen on it. People could send emails, watch TV, or pay bills on this screen. However, most people's internet connection speeds were still quite slow. For most people, IoT technology wasn't very useful yet.

The IoT really took off when Apple released the iPhone in 2007. Using this smartphone, people could access the internet from almost anywhere. They finally had a convenient way to connect to and control other devices online. Before long, millions of people owned smartphones. The number of other internet-connected objects also grew. By 2008, there were more connected items than humans in the world.

KEVIN ASHTON

Kevin Ashton is known as the Father of the Internet of Things. He coined the term *Internet of Things* in 1999 while working for Procter & Gamble. This company makes personal care products, such as soap, toothpaste, and lipstick.

Ashton's job was selling cosmetics. He noticed a problem. Popular products sold out quickly. Then the store's shelves sat empty until the next week's delivery. People couldn't buy the products they wanted, and the store lost money.

Around this time, some stores began offering loyalty cards. Each card held a tiny microchip that could transfer data. The cards gave Ashton an idea. By placing a chip on a product, his company could track its location. Each store could tell how many products were on its shelves. When its stock of popular products got low, the store could order more. It would no longer run out.

▲ Kevin Ashton holds an RFID tag that companies can use to track their products.

Ashton teamed up with scientists at the Massachusetts Institute of Technology to test his idea. They made RFID tags that could attach to products. Ashton told other companies about the tags. As interest grew, the chips got cheaper and easier to make. Today, stores around the world use this technology to track their products.

CHAPTER 3

HOW THE IoT WORKS

All IoT devices use the internet to send and receive information. In order to do this, an object needs an internet protocol (IP) address. Like a mailing address tells the post office where to send a letter, an IP address tells computers where to send information. The address also tells computers where the information is coming from. That way, the information will go to and from the correct devices.

Each device that connects to the internet receives an IP address.

An IP address is assigned when a device connects to a network. Devices connect to the internet and to one another in different ways. Some use wires. Others use wireless technology. Wireless devices can use a variety of methods to send and receive information. Some use satellites. Others use cell phone networks, Wi-Fi, or Bluetooth.

Each device uses sensors to record information about the world around it. Some sensors measure temperature, light, pressure, or vibrations. Others take pictures, record sounds, or measure speed. Sensors may track an object's position or show how close it is to other objects. The sensors send this data to the network.

RFID tags are a common type of sensor. Each RFID tag includes a microchip. This chip sends out radio signals. An RFID reader picks them up.

RFID tags stick to products such as clothing.

RFID readers can keep track of information from many objects at once. And wireless networks make it easy for them to connect to the internet in almost any location. As RFID technology improves, the tags are becoming smaller and cheaper. Even tiny items can be part of the IoT.

Smart devices use computer programs to send and receive information. All programs run on some kind of **platform**. Every platform is unique.

It can use only certain programs and languages. Early IoT devices often used different platforms. As a result, they could not work together.

By the mid-1990s, cloud computing helped solve this problem. The cloud is a group of services and platforms that can be used on any internet-connected device. It makes connections between devices simpler and faster. It also provides space to store all the data they collect.

In the future, computer programs may help control devices. Some may even act without instructions from a person. Devices already use artificial intelligence (AI). AI is the science of

➤ THINK ABOUT IT

Billions of devices are part of the IoT. What challenges could managing data from so many devices create?

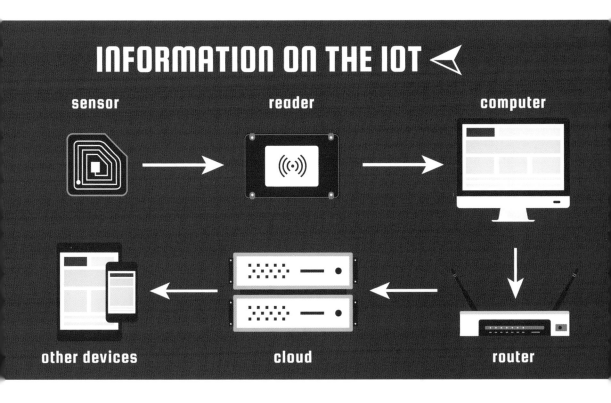

INFORMATION ON THE IOT

sensor

reader

computer

other devices

cloud

router

creating machines that can act like humans. For example, in a process called machine learning, computers are trained to find patterns in data. Machine learning can help study and organize the data IoT devices collect. Computers can identify the useful data and take action. For instance, a thermostat that uses AI could adjust a home's temperature based on the family's normal activity.

CHAPTER 4

ALL KINDS OF DEVICES

For many people, IoT devices have become part of everyday life. These devices often work together. For example, a house might have several smart appliances. It may use a smart home hub to connect the devices and control them. The hub handles the data the devices collect. It helps them send and receive information. Many hubs allow people to control their devices using an app. A hub may also connect the devices to the cloud.

Amazon's Echo Plus (center) can act as a smart home hub.

Some homes have smart speakers. Users can ask these speakers to play music or videos on connected devices. Some smart speakers work with virtual assistants. These computer programs use AI to perform tasks that can be done over the internet. They can check sports scores, order food, find recipes, and more.

Another popular IoT device is the fitness tracker. Usually worn on the wrist, this device counts the number of steps a person takes. It can connect to treadmills, exercise bikes, and scales. It collects and shares data with these machines. For example, it can track the calories the person burns. Trackers can display all this information for users. They can even monitor users' sleep patterns.

Some stores use IoT technology instead of cashiers. Shoppers log in with their phones, put

▲ Apple's Siri is one example of a virtual assistant.

items in their cart, and walk out the door. Cameras and weight sensors on the store's shelves track the products. RFID tags on the products help, too. They send information to an electronic reader. The reader records the items each shopper chooses. Then it charges the person's credit card.

IoT devices can also track customers. Cameras and sensors can be placed throughout the store.

▲ Ceiling cameras allow stores to study customers' buying habits.

These devices help the store map how shoppers walk through the aisles. This information helps workers choose where to put new products or sale items. Some stores also use beacons. These devices send out messages. Each beacon can tell when a smartphone is nearby. It sends a coupon or notice to the phone.

Even plants and animals are being connected to the IoT. Lumber companies can tag trees using RFID tags. The tag records information about the tree, such as its watering schedule. And after the tree is cut and sold, GPS can show the lumber's location.

Many animals now have RFID tags as well. The tags let farmers track their animals' location. They can also track each animal's health and food intake. This helps farmers keep their animals healthy and cut down on waste. RFID tags can also help people find and identify lost pets.

The IoT can help travelers, too. People who often drive on toll roads can buy a pass. Tollbooths record signals from a **transponder** when the car goes by. The driver does not need to stop. Instead, the booths charge the correct fee automatically. This process saves time.

CHAPTER 5

EFFICIENT SYSTEMS

As technology improves, more and more things are becoming connected. The IoT now includes not only appliances but also airplane engines and scientific tools. In fact, many industries use the IoT to stay safe or earn more money.

For example, manufacturers can use smart sensors to help process their products. Some sensors detect when supplies are getting low.

Sensors in jet engines can monitor pressure, temperature, and fuel levels as a plane flies.

Companies can order more supplies before they run out. Other sensors keep an eye on equipment to make sure it is working properly. They can send an alert when the equipment needs to be cleaned or replaced. That way, repairs can be made before the equipment breaks down.

The IoT also helps with energy production. For example, wind farms use giant windmills to generate electricity. Sensors monitor the wind's speed and direction. Computers use this data to turn each windmill so it will catch the most wind. This helps the wind farm produce up to 25 percent more energy. That way, the power company earns more money.

IoT devices play a huge role in modern medicine. In fact, many lifesaving treatments now rely on the IoT. Pacemakers help keep a person's heart beating in rhythm. Other devices monitor

⬆ The IoT can help make wind farms more efficient at harnessing wind energy.

glucose levels, activity, and sleep. They share this data with the patient's doctor. Medical staff can monitor and control these devices via the internet. Some devices remind people when to take medicine. They can alert a medical team if something is wrong.

The IoT also makes it easy to store and share patient records. Machines such as X-rays can take digital images and share them with doctors. AI programs may read and interpret the images before the doctor sees them. The programs help diagnose diseases. In some cases, AI is better at finding diseased tissue than human workers are.

Scientists can even use the IoT to track the spread of viruses. This can help control disease. In Brazil, for example, scientists watch for outbreaks of Zika. This virus is spread by mosquitoes. Smart thermometers can help detect an outbreak. They send patients' temperatures to a global system. If an area shows an increase in fevers, the Zika virus may be spreading there. Scientists also use sensors to track an area's temperature and weather. They hope this data will help them learn about how the virus spreads.

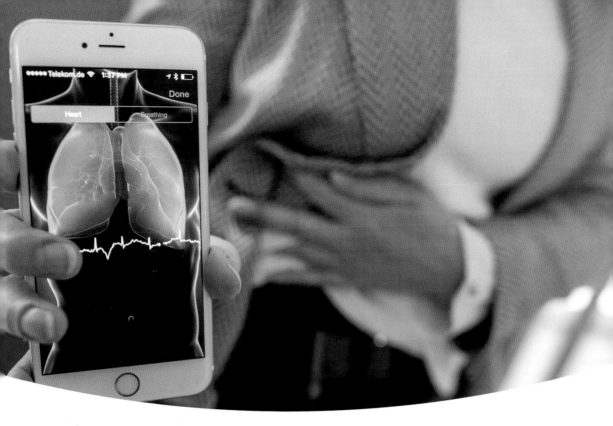

A woman wears a shirt that uses sensors to track her breathing and pulse.

These are just a few of many ways the IoT can help doctors and nurses take better care of patients. One day, people may wear sensors on or inside their bodies. The sensors could monitor their vital signs or make sure people received the proper amount of medicine. **Nanobots** might alert medical teams if something was wrong.

LARISSA ROMUALDO SUZUKI

Dr. Larissa Romualdo Suzuki is a computer scientist. Ever since she was a child, she has loved studying electronics and machines. Born in Brazil, Suzuki studied computer science and electrical engineering. She has worked on many projects related to smart cities and the IoT. For one project, Suzuki created a data infrastructure plan for the city of London, England.

Infrastructure is the basic structure of a society. It includes things such as roads, sewers, and power lines. Cities work hard to keep these systems running smoothly. But they often face problems such as traffic jams or power outages.

The IoT gives cities access to huge amounts of information about these systems and the people who use them. Sensors, cameras, smartphones,

⬧ Dr. Suzuki created a system to monitor and organize data about the city of London.

and many other devices collect and share data all the time.

Data infrastructure focuses on finding the best way to organize that information. Organized data is easier to study. Suzuki planned to show how people used London's systems as well as the problems those users faced. Her project aimed to solve these problems and save the city money. It identified technologies that could make the city's systems more efficient. And it helped the systems work together.

CHAPTER 6

NEW CHALLENGES

The IoT offers many benefits. But like any new technology, it has risks. Security is a huge concern. IoT devices collect lots of information. Only the devices on a network and their users should have access to that data. But sometimes other people can gain access.

Many people worry that **hackers** will see their data. Hackers often gain access to a computer network through the devices connected to it.

Hackers might attempt to access other people's devices through the IoT.

The more devices that are connected to the network, the greater the risk of hacking. An IoT network can contain many devices. And these devices are often not very secure. Hackers have gained access to cameras and baby monitors. Even a toy robot could open the door to a hacker.

Once a hacker reaches the network, he or she can access the information it contains. This can include passwords, banking information, email accounts, and more. A hacker could steal a person's money or identity.

Other times, hackers cause a device to stop working properly. For instance, they could cause a car's brakes to fail. Or they could damage a medical device, such as a pacemaker. The person using the device could be seriously hurt or killed. Hackers could even take control of a building or computer network.

Sometimes hackers try to infect a whole network of devices with **malware**. They can use these networks, called **botnets**, to send spam messages, shut down websites, or show ads.

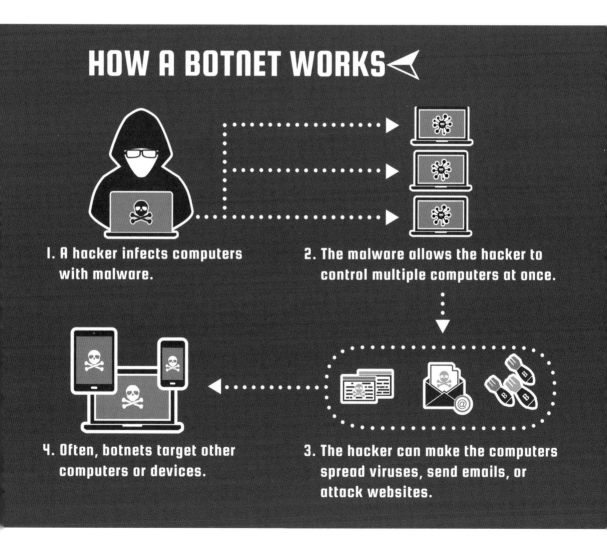

HOW A BOTNET WORKS

1. A hacker infects computers with malware.

2. The malware allows the hacker to control multiple computers at once.

3. The hacker can make the computers spread viruses, send emails, or attack websites.

4. Often, botnets target other computers or devices.

Botnets have caused websites such as Amazon and Netflix to crash. Not being able to access websites is annoying to users. But if hackers target a government network or **public utility**, they can cause much greater harm. In 2015, for example, a power plant in Ukraine was hacked. Around 80,000 people lost power. Governments work hard to guard against this type of attack.

Families can also take steps to keep their devices safe from hackers. Experts recommend setting up a separate Wi-Fi network just for IoT devices. This network should have its own password. Changing passwords every three or four months can also help prevent hacks.

Privacy is another big concern with the IoT. Smart devices collect huge amounts of data about the people who use them. They monitor people's driving habits, health, location, and

A wireless router sends out signals to create a Wi-Fi network.

more. The more information the devices collect, the more useful they can be. But many people are concerned about what happens to this information. Users have little control over what companies do with it. For instance, companies could access the data without asking permission. Or they might sell a person's information to advertisers. IoT users should read the privacy information for each device. That way, they can adjust how much information they want to share.

CHAPTER 7

THE FUTURE OF THE IoT

The IoT continues to grow and expand. Soon, devices may use it to share even more kinds of information. One company is developing smartphones that can detect flavors and smells. These phones could help keep their users safe. For example, a phone could tell when someone has had too much alcohol to drive. It could prevent the person's car from turning on. In addition, a phone could detect when food is contaminated.

One day, the IoT may help people care for pets.

If the food container had an RFID tag, the phone could notify the company that made the food. The company could remove the food from stores before more people got sick.

Cities are an ideal place for IoT technology to expand. Scientists have started designing smart city grids. Each grid is like a smart home hub, but for an entire city. It helps control the city's systems. For instance, the grid might control the city's stoplights to help traffic flow. Or it might communicate with smart cars. It could help them find new routes to avoid accidents or construction. Humans would no longer have to control the route.

➤ THINK ABOUT IT

Other than cars and traffic, what parts of life in a city could the IoT improve?

Stoplights could adjust the length of time they stay red to keep traffic moving.

As IoT technology improves, devices will be able to do more and more on their own. They may begin anticipating what people need. A refrigerator could sense when it started getting empty and order more groceries. A drone could deliver the food right to the house. Other companies could use drones to deliver packages. Thanks to inventions such as these, the IoT will continue to make people's lives easier.

FOCUS ON THE
INTERNET OF THINGS

Write your answers on a separate piece of paper.

1. Write a paragraph summarizing the two main challenges described in Chapter 6.

2. Would you want to live in a home where all the appliances are controlled by a smart home hub and virtual assistant? Why or why not?

3. Which sensor can attach to objects to help stores track their products?

    A. a GPS satellite
    B. an RFID tag
    C. an RFID reader

4. How could the IoT help a smart city grid improve traffic flow?

    A. The grid could look for areas with heavy traffic and send cars around them.
    B. The grid could find the shortest distance and send all cars along that route.
    C. The grid could keep an equal amount of space between all cars on the road.

Answer key on page 48.

GLOSSARY

botnets
Groups of computers or other devices that have been infected by malware that allows a hacker to control all of them at once.

glucose
A sugar found in plants that is converted to energy by the body.

GPS receiver
A device that picks up signals from several GPS satellites and uses the locations of those satellites to calculate its own location.

hackers
People who illegally access computers or other devices.

malware
Computer programs intended for a bad purpose.

nanobots
Tiny robots that are small enough to go inside the body.

network
A system of computers and devices that are connected to one another.

platform
A basic set of hardware and software that allows a computer program to run.

public utility
An organization that provides a service to a community, such as supplying gas, electricity, or water.

transponder
A device that receives a radio signal and automatically sends out another signal.

TO LEARN MORE

BOOKS

Duke, Shirley. *Information Waves*. Vero Beach, FL: Rourke Educational Media, 2016.

Hand, Carol. *How the Internet Changed History*. Minneapolis: Abdo Publishing, 2015.

January, Brendan. *Information Insecurity: Privacy Under Siege*. Minneapolis: Twenty-First Century Books, 2016.

NOTE TO EDUCATORS

Visit **www.focusreaders.com** to find lesson plans, activities, links, and other resources related to this title.

INDEX

artificial intelligence (AI), 20–21, 24, 32

bar codes, 10, 12

cloud computing, 20–21, 23

data infrastructure, 34–35

fitness tracker, 24

GPS, 10–11, 13, 27

hackers, 37–40

IP address, 17–18

malware, 39
medicine, 30–31, 33

network, 6–7, 18–19, 37–40

privacy, 40–41

RFID tags, 12–13, 15, 18–19, 25, 27, 44

satellites, 11, 18
security, 37–38
sensors, 6, 18, 21, 25, 29–30, 32–33, 34
smart cities, 34–35, 44
smart home hub, 23, 44
smartphones, 5–7, 13, 24, 26, 34, 43–44
stores, 9–10, 14–15, 24–26, 44

Answer Key: 1. Answers will vary; **2.** Answers will vary; **3.** B; **4.** A